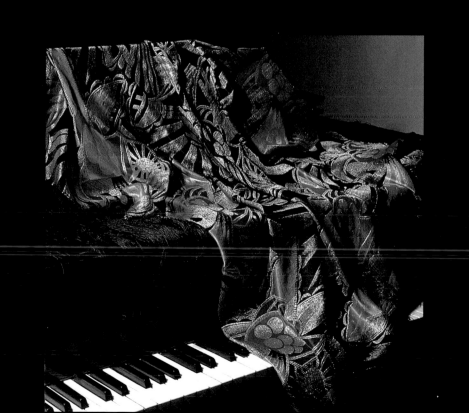

"Roses sur Paris"
de
Christian Dior

The Scarf

Andrew Baseman

Text by Harold Carlton
Photographs by Robin Nedboy

Stewart, Tabori & Chang
New York

FOR MOM AND DAD

Page 1: An Art Deco shawl with metallic threads and fringed border (French, late 1920s).

Page 2: "Roses sur Paris" (French, mid-1950s).

Page 3: Hermès' "Sangles."

This page, clockwise from lower left: "Reno Sweeney from *Anything Goes*," by James McMullan (1988); "Meilleurs Voeux!" designed by Marc Bohan (French, c. 1960); a still life with scarf.

Opposite, clockwise from lower left: a hand-painted scarf by Michael Tellin (American, 1970); a hand-batiked scarf inspired by Tiffany windows (American, 1920s); "Dragon" by Georgina von Etzdorf (English, 1982); a model in a scarf by Jacques Heim (French, c. 1957).

Published in 1989 by
Stewart, Tabori & Chang, Inc.
740 Broadway, New York, New York 10003

Library of Congress Cataloging-in-Publication Data
Baseman, Andrew.
   The scarf / Andrew Baseman ; text by Harold Carlton ; photographs by Robin Nedboy.
      p.   cm.
   ISBN 1-55670-061-X : $30.00
   1. Scarves.   I. Title.
GT2113.B37   1989   89-30648
391'.41—dc19   CIP

Distributed in the U.S. by Workman Publishing,
708 Broadway, New York, New York 10003
Distributed in Canada by Canadian Manda Group,
P.O. Box 920 Station U, Toronto, Ontario M8Z 5P9
Distributed in all other territories by Little, Brown & Company,
International Division, 34 Beacon Street, Boston, MA 02108

Printed in Japan
10 9 8 7 6 5 4 3 2 1

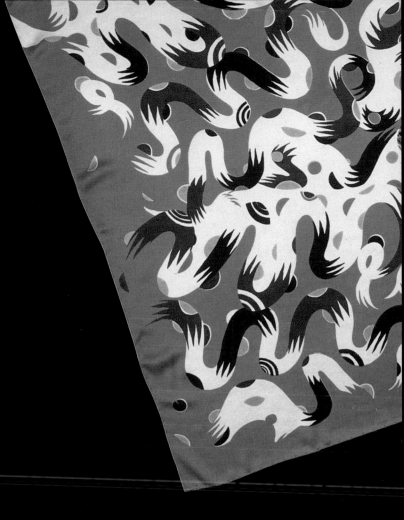

Contents

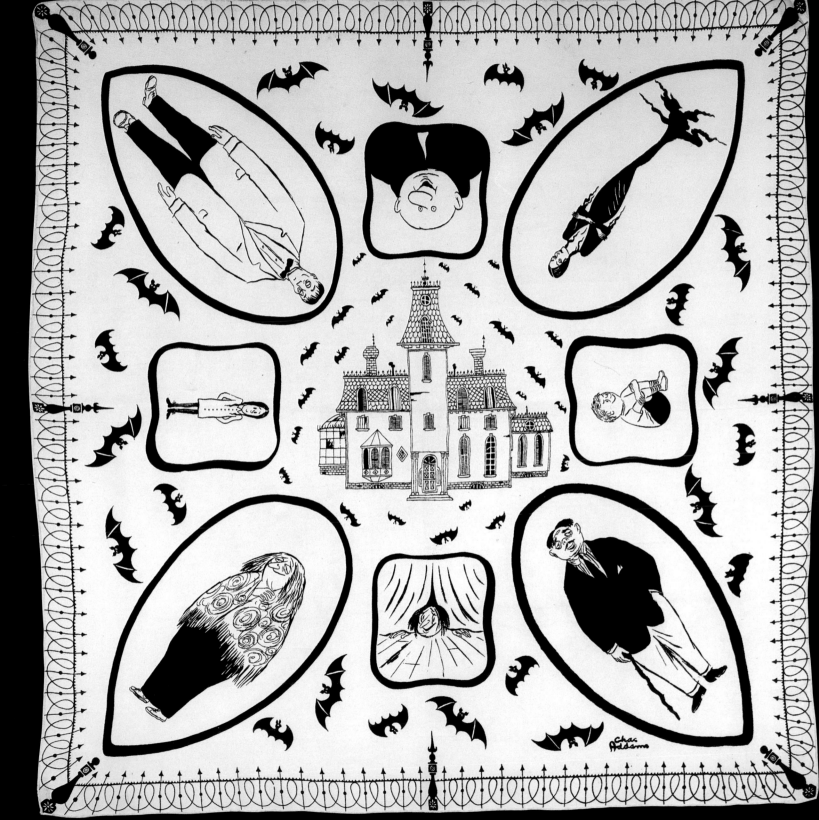

Foreword

*I*n the spring of 1979, I purchased my first scarf. It was signed by Charles Addams, and it depicted characters from his New Yorker cartoons. I uncovered this accessory at a vintage clothing store in Pittsburgh during my freshman year at college. At first, I had no idea why I was buying this item; I wasn't going to wear it, nor was I going to give it as a gift. But there was something enticing about this silk square. Maybe it was a sudden surge of nostalgia for the television show "The Addams Family" from the 1960s. Or maybe I was drawn to the billowy feel of the silk. In any case, I bought the scarf and hung it on my wall, where it received much attention and inspired many requests to be worn. This article of clothing became an object of art, to be viewed like a painting or to be worn as a fashion accessory.

I found most of the scarves shown in this book during the ten years of collecting that followed this first purchase. Throughout this time, I have taken delight in the endless search for more examples of these graphic silk canvases.

The scarves reproduced on the following pages do not pretend to constitute a scholarly history of the printed scarf. They do trace the transformation of the scarf through the twentieth century, but always with the thought of the scarf as wearable art. I hope you enjoy the rediscovery of this always loved, but often neglected, garment.

Andrew Baseman

Opposite: Scarf by Charles Addams, commissioned by Richard Farrar (American, c. 1951).

The Magic of the Scarf

*T*he magician performs his practiced flourish and suddenly produces a fluttering white dove or a bouquet of colored paper flowers from . . . a silk scarf!

This is only the first bit of magic that a scarf can work. Watch a woman with her scarf. Watch her handle it, play with it, crumple it, and finally hold it aloft, folded into a triangle, and bring it down over her head, covering her hair, tying it under her chin. Watch her as she loosens her scarf, lets it slide off her head, and shakes out her hair. What special powers does this silk square possess? Does it incorporate some of the mystique of the bride's veil, the nun's habit, the nurse's coif, the Arab woman's yashmak? You might well answer yes to all this, and you might also come up with other ideas of your own. For the scarf is so much more than a simple square to be worn on the head, around the neck, draped from a shoulder, tied at the waist. It can be a touch of frivolity, an elegant accessory, a brilliantly colored, beautifully designed objet d'art *suitable for framing.*

In her Guide to Vintage Chic, *Harriet Love rhapsodizes: "My scarf collection numbers fifty. Most are so beautiful that I take them out to admire them more often than I wear them. I feel as though I own fifty paintings all hidden away." That's what we hope you'll feel about scarves after reading this book.*

Opposite: Marlene Dietrich, in *The Garden of Allah* (1936).

The History of the Scarf

The scarf as we know it was born with the new century. Lady Hamilton's shawl dances may well have hypnotized Goethe during the eighteenth century, and the Romantics of the nineteenth century may have ascribed special properties to shawls because they "framed the heart of the wearer." But not until the twentieth century did the scarf assume its rightful place as a vital accessory in every woman's wardrobe. The influences that were to make the scarf popular emerged in the 1880s, when two American dancers conquered Paris. Then an entire ballet troupe brought sweeping visual changes to the art world and, as these changes filtered down into everyday life, to women's fashion.

Loie Fuller, an American who debuted at the Folies Bergères with her novelty dance act, used long scarflike lengths of fabric stitched to wands, their rippling shapes illuminated by colored lights. Toulouse-Lautrec was inspired

The mystique Loie Fuller created while dancing with scarves inspired artists to capture her in posters, painting, and statuary.

to paint her again and again during the late 1880s, producing posters advertising her act. And Art Nouveau statuettes depict her, scarves caught in the air.

Isadora Duncan specialized in free-form paeans to freedom—freedom of spirit as well as of movement. When she danced, Duncan gloried in the dramatic effect of yards of "Grecian" draping flowing out behind her. She would suddenly stop, turn to the audience, and stretch her arms upward in supplication or triumph as her draperies rippled to a standstill at her feet, settling artistically like the ornamentation around the dais of a classical statue.

By the time the chorus of the Ballets Russes added scarves to elongate its movements in such exotic sensuous ballets as Scheherazade (1910) and Nijinsky had toyed seductively with a scarf in L'après-midi d'un faune (1912), the fashion-conscious had received the message: long, draped pieces of fabric—preferably silk—added a chic, slightly untamed look to slinky dresses and tailored outfits. Thus the scarf began this century entwining its way sinuously and decoratively around the fashion drawings, pochoirs,

Opposite: While couturiers played with the pairing of scarves and tailored outfits, artists and photographers were often more fascinated with scarves draped on the nude.

and fantasies of Mucha, Benito, and Lepape. The scarf was versatile, able to echo the serpentine twists of Art Nouveau and yet also to herald the straight lines of Art Deco.

But it was a few years earlier, in 1906, that the scarf's success had been assured. In that year, Paris hairdressers discovered the permanent wave. An orgy of cutting, shingling, bobbing, and perming resulted, producing a small, short, neat head, a head ready for a scarf!

In Gazette du Bon Ton, a French fashion magazine, long, flowing scarves added chic and graphic zip to the languid, elongated styles that presaged the 1920s. On a 1913 menu cover for the Savoy Hotel, fashion artist Georges Lepape suggested how important scarves were to become. Around the head of a dancing woman in a white pleated crepe dress, he wrapped a black silk scarf that covered her ears and chin and billowed out exuberantly for yards behind her.

An American Vogue cover of 1918, again illustrated by Le-

SERENELY POISED UPON THE VERY PINNACLE OF CHIC IS THE GAY YOUNG PERSON WHO HAS SCALED THE DIFFICULT HEIGHTS OF THE NEW SIMPLICITY . . . HER CONTRASTING COLORS ARE EVOLVED BY STEHLI

Stehli Silks

An advertisement for the American company Stehli Silks (1929).

pape, also promoted the scarf. A white woolen fringed scarf that appeared to be 35 feet long was thrown around and around the neck of a leaping, green-redingoted girl. It was a fashion artist's exaggeration, but it was a prophetic indication of the direction scarves were about to take.

By 1921, Dress Essentials magazine was proclaiming, "The sports scarf is an increasingly important article in neckwear design," and advertisements showed "lustrous fibre silk scarves," calling them "quaintly amusing" and listing their colors as "pearl gray, terra cotta, and chocolate." Illustra-

tions showed thick scarves, long and fringed, worn around the neck to hang, sometimes belted, to the hips. Cecil Beaton portrayed the legendary Mrs. Harrison Williams as she stood beneath a tall palm tree in Palm Beach wearing a plain white streak of a dress and a long multicolored striped silk scarf hanging simply, untied, around her neck.

Sonia Delaunay was one of the Paris artists who worked in the realm where art and fashion overlapped, as they did for a while. In 1924, she produced some of the most beautiful scarves ever seen. Embroidered, appliquéd, hand-painted, these scarves were like long, abstract paintings, up to 6 feet long and 18 inches wide. Their designs echoed those of the Bauhaus, even Matisse. Some of Delaunay's creations were black and white; others were in pastels with vivid purples or a whole rainbow of daring new colors. They were worn over long gowns and allowed to hang or glide carelessly. They were, in fact, a little bohemian, an early version of the "rich hippie" look; they hinted that the wearer was an original, a little different, perhaps just slightly wild.

Coco Chanel's creations were breathlessly featured by an adoring press. In 1924, Vogue featured one of her skirts unbuttoned over crepe pantalettes, along with a tiny cloche hat and a big black silk scarf flapping madly in the wind whipped up by the studio fan.

Fashionable Dress, an American publication, stated in its June 1929 issue: "Silk scarves, because of the rational saneness behind them, are going to be very popular. You will see them at mountain resorts where cool nights invite them. They are also going to the beaches where capricious breezes make them most welcome." The editorial ended confidently: "Each of us will want to own a scarf ensemble."

The Surrealist movement—and the creations of its fashion monarch, Elsa Schiaparelli—also contributed to the scarf's evolution. Schiaparelli's "triple scarves" in red, white, and

A Georges Lepape cover for American *Vogue* (June 1, 1925).

blue—nationalistic colors for both the Americans and the French—were just one example of her rethinking the common scarf. Charles James, the innovative American couturier, also affected the early 1930s with his "twisted endless tubes," worn in different-colored pairs at the neck, on the head, or at the

waist. James was fascinated by the scarf and often reinvented it. He designed a trumpet-shaped scarf composed of wedges of ribbon, a lappetlike scarf with rounded ends and a bulbous central form, and a scarf with a narrow neckback and triangular flared ends.

Paris couturiers such as

Chanel, Patou, Fath, and Worth had slowly begun to introduce scarves bearing their name in the 1930s. Sold from their boutiques and in certain prestigious department stores, these scarves proved to be a useful form of advertising. And a silk scarf with the griffe of a famous couturier was often the only affordable luxury item for the woman who craved a Paris label on at least one item of clothing; it was the precursor of today's designer labels.

The Second World War brought the scarf down to a more utilitarian level as women went to work in ammunition and aircraft factories and had to protect their long hair from moving machinery. But scarves at this time served other purposes, too. During the First World War, some handkerchief manufacturers had printed sentimental, patriotic images on their wares. These squares carried such sad verses and showed such pretty nurses, grieving mothers, and stalwart young soldiers that no sooner had you read your hanky than you began to cry into it. During the

Second World War, scarves replaced handkerchiefs, and this time the mood was not so sentimental. It was considered patriotic as well as morale-building to wear cheery slogans or rousing phrases from Winston Churchill's speeches over your head or around your neck. In England, Jacqmar Scarves produced a series of booster headscarves in bright, optimistic primary colors. One showed a brick wall plastered with colored bills reading "Save for Victory"; "Go! To! It!"; "Lend to Defend the Right to Be Free!"; and "Bill Stickers Will Be Prosecuted by Jacqmar" as a cheeky way of signing the scarf. Jacqmar was the first British manufacturer to build its own name label and proudly display it on its scarves. This firm was begun by Joseph H. Lyons in 1935, after he had spent twenty years supplying silks to London's couture houses. After the war, Jacqmar's colorful silk scarves became a symbol of the new luxury and choice the fashion-starved British hoped they could now look forward to.

The majority of the commemorative scarves from the Second World War were made by English and American companies. This 1949 Dutch scarf entitled "Prinses Irene" chronicles the war effort in Holland.

Many scarf collectors concentrate on this historically rich period when scarves were printed especially for the captive market of servicemen shopping for light, easy-to-mail, and inexpensive gifts. Due to shortages of raw materials these wartime scarves were usually printed on acetates or synthetic fabrics.

In 1937, Hermès, the harness-makers, had printed the first of millions of its horsey scarves, little dreaming that one day its carrés would account for most of its business. The firm of Gucci, founded as a saddle-maker's by Guccio Gucci in Florence in 1906, did not follow Hermès' lead until 1953, when it sold its first scarves from a tiny boutique in New York's St. Regis Hotel. Although sometimes using an equestrian motif and the GG initials of its founder, it evolved its own clean-cut floral styles and now takes great pride in the fact that up to fifty-one screens have been used to print its intense, vibrant scarves.

Other 1950s purveyors of the scarf included the austere Brooke Cadwallader, whose "Bronzini" line of menswear was particularly noteworthy, and the whimsical Tammis Keefe, whose creations are now cultish collector's items.

The 1960s began calmly enough. In Europe, "scarf-hats"—silk scarves over straw shapes—were the rage. Vogue showed Jean Shrimpton wearing one on its August 1963 cover. But the "Youthquake" that began with the British Invasion of 1964—spearheaded by the Beatles, Mary Quant, and Twiggy, among others—changed the look of clothing. The scarf had its own revolution, led by Vera Neumann, Peter Max, and the Marchese Pucci Barsento (Emilio Pucci). This odd trio, who could not

Opposite: An unusual collection of cotton commemorative scarves.

have come from more diverse backgrounds or been more artistically dissimilar, popularized the scarf in the 1960s, and, for one brief and shining moment, their designs shared the same glowing neon hues, the same acid rainbow of colors, the same psychedelic patterns. Gradually, they found different markets, Max appealing to the "flower children," Pucci to the suddenly label-conscious, and Vera, who had first introduced her eponymous line in the late 1940s, to the middle-of-the-roaders.

In the 1960s, one chose between the long, bias-cut 1930s scarves that the truly hip wore with their antique clothing and the neat, clean-cut looks of Quant, Courrèges, and Ungaro. Never before had fashion forced people into such pigeonholes. Female Youthquakers wore Vera or Pucci squares very properly over the head or at the neck, and they tied Hermes scarves to

Opposite: A trio of scarves from English designer Georgina von Etzdorf. Shown are "Moonfish," 1976 (upper left), "Bonfire," 1988 (upper right and lower left), and "Rocket," 1988.

An exceptional colorist, Jean Patou was almost as well known for his scarves as for his gowns.

their purse handles. Hippies of both sexes wore antique or Peter Max scarves, free-flowing from the neck or tied as bandeaux around the forehead like 1920s flappers. It was now "Them" versus "Us," and fashion—including scarves—reflected this division accordingly.

In the 1970s, Ferragamo, an Italian shoe firm that had achieved success in the early 1950s, entered the scarf business and cornered the "jungle market." Its large silk squares boasted vivid depictions of leopards, tigers, and exotic, tropical foliage.

Today, the prospects for the scarf look brighter than ever. Scarf-consciousness has never been so evident in advertising, in stores, in everyday life.

One of the most striking of today's designers is Georgina von Etzdorf, who works out of an old barn in Wiltshire, England, with her two partners. Her silk fabrics have been used in clothes for the Princess of Wales, and a 1982 British Vogue cover put her on the fashion map. Von Etzdorf's fresh and strangely beautiful designs blend serious, deep, vivid colors and quirky, playful, lively patterns.

For their Fall 1988 collections, the world's designers acknowledged the importance of the scarf as never before. Rei Kawakubo of Comme des Garçons, generally regarded as today's most prophetic designer, tied scarves on the heads of most of her female models and around the necks of their male counterparts. Italian designers Giorgio Armani and Gianni Versace also both showed scarves.

Tiffany, the long-established jewelry store, once known for its exquisite lamps, then for its award-winning window displays, also entered the Great Scarf Race in 1988, when it introduced a score of abstract florals and two "stained glass" patterns by one of its vice-presidents, Gene Moore, designer of the Tiffany windows. Louis Vuitton, who for many years had produced only one monogrammed brown scarf to match its luggage, suddenly commissioned five artists, including James Rosenquist, to design scarves in 1988 as well.

Woman's Wear Daily, in

their coverage of the Paris collections for spring 1989, advises, "Forget baubles and trinkets. The only accessory to collect by the dozen next spring is the scarf." So one can expect to see every size of scarf worn in the future, from 30-inch squares to the oversized 60-inch "throws" or "falls" that many women seem to have adopted as security blankets and as a dramatic way to keep one shoulder warm. As we stand on the brink of the 1990s, it seems clear that the scarf has yet to reach its peak.

Top left: Also in the line of Tiffany scarves are these examples designed by Tiffany Design Director John Loring (American, 1988).

Left: A detail from Gucci's "Safari" (Italian, 1969). Fifty separate silk screens were used to create the rich coloring and detail.

Opposite: Another offering from Tiffany & Co., this entitled "Edwardian" (American, 1988).

Isadora

Isadora Duncan, who gave dance a new direction in the last quarter of the nineteenth century, died on September 14, 1927, a victim of the long, dramatic scarves she loved to wear. She had popularized loose, trailing draperies, which she used to add movement and excitement to her dances. In real life, too, she was a larger-than-life figure who adored shawls, stoles, and scarves. The night she died, she was taking a trial run in the scarlet Bugatti of an Italian friend, Benoit Falchetto. Although living in near-poverty in a seedy Côte d'Azur hotel, she was thinking of buying the car from him.

She had prepared for the drive in a heavy red cashmere Marseillaise shawl, but, never one to underdress, she put on another long, silk-fringed scarf at the last minute. As the car took off, she turned to friends and called out prophetically, "Adieu mes amis, je vais a la gloire!" ("Farewell, my friends,

Isadora Duncan, "just arrived in New York, going to South America to dance" (c. 1925).

Right: Vanessa Redgrave in *Isadora: "Adieu mes amis, je vais à la gloire!"*

I'm off to glory.") She threw the long-fringed end of the shawl, wound tightly around her throat, over her left shoulder. The car started forward; then it stopped. Her friends saw her head jerk back, then fall and remain quite still. The scarf and its fringes were bound up in the spokes and hub of the front wheel. With several turns and one swift, accelerated blow, her larynx had been crushed, her neck broken, her carotid artery burst. It was the final act of an extraordinary life.

Opposite: Redgrave captured Isadora's freedom of movement, echoed by the fluid motion of the scarf.

Cowboys and Gentlemen

Long before cowboys and Indians were considered subjects for entertainment, cowboy neckerchiefs were called "wipes." Used to mop sweat and grime from faces and necks, wipes proved that the Old West had no time for the niceties of life. Deliberately dark or dull, kerchiefs had to blend in with the background of the hot, dusty range, camouflaging the cowboy from danger. The sunburnt far-from-chic cowboy had no inkling that a century later he would be an American fashion prototype. It took pulp novels, movies, and

finally television to elevate the cowboy into a romantic "fashion statement."

The first Western movie (Cripple Creek Barroom, 1898) tapped an insatiable thirst for Western entertainment. After that, cowboy stars were off and running. Thanks to lurid magazine and comic-book covers, along with cleverly merchandised clothing and novelties, the neckerchief evolved by the 1920s into a colorful, decorative men's accessory. Although called a neckerchief, it was very often a voluminous, full-blown scarf.

Wearing a neckerchief was one way of identifying with your cowboy idol. Even better was wearing a neckerchief endorsed by the star. Scarf manufacturers were happy to oblige. An early offering was from Tom Mix, self-proclaimed "King of the Cowboys." His 1920s radio show offered the Tom Mix bandanna for a box top (from Ralston Cereal) and a dime. It showed the star on horseback amid a border of cacti, steers' heads,

and coiled ropes, the "TM" logo in each corner. You could also get a live baby turtle—branded!

For fans of the Lone Ranger, an official Lone Ranger linen neckerchief was available—red, black, and white, it showed him on his horse. And Gene Autry merchandise included watches, galoshes, lunchboxes, and Thermos flasks, as well as a satin-rayon neckerchief with a border of guns, horseshoes, lassos, boots, and spurs.

William S. Hart, star of realistic Westerns that were as successful as they were influential, insisted on accuracy in his costumes. Here, he wears two bandanas. Other stars, such as Gary Cooper (*left*) and Bing Crosby (*opposite*) captured other facets of the romance of the West. But whoever the star, he wore a scarf.

Opposite: Inspired by the movies, this scarf—entitled "Ride 'Em Cowboy"—is packed with every Western cliché imaginable (American, c. 1935).

Left: The scarf was an unusually delicate accessory for a cowboy, but it was also worn by men, women, and children across the United States. Here are three examples from the 1930s: a silk neckerchief entitled "The Round Up—Let 'Er Buck," a cotton bandana with a silver figural scarf slide, and a simple red cotton bandana.

Overleaf left: Interest in things Western continued into the 1970s. This is a Roy Lichtenstein-inspired design for the Fiorucci stores (Italian, c. 1975).

Overleaf right: The classic cotton bandanas *(upper left and lower right)* from the 1920s were perhaps inspired by silk handkerchiefs, such as this 1870 example *(upper right)*. Their timeless patterns are quite different from the often kitschy figures of the 1930s *(lower left)*.

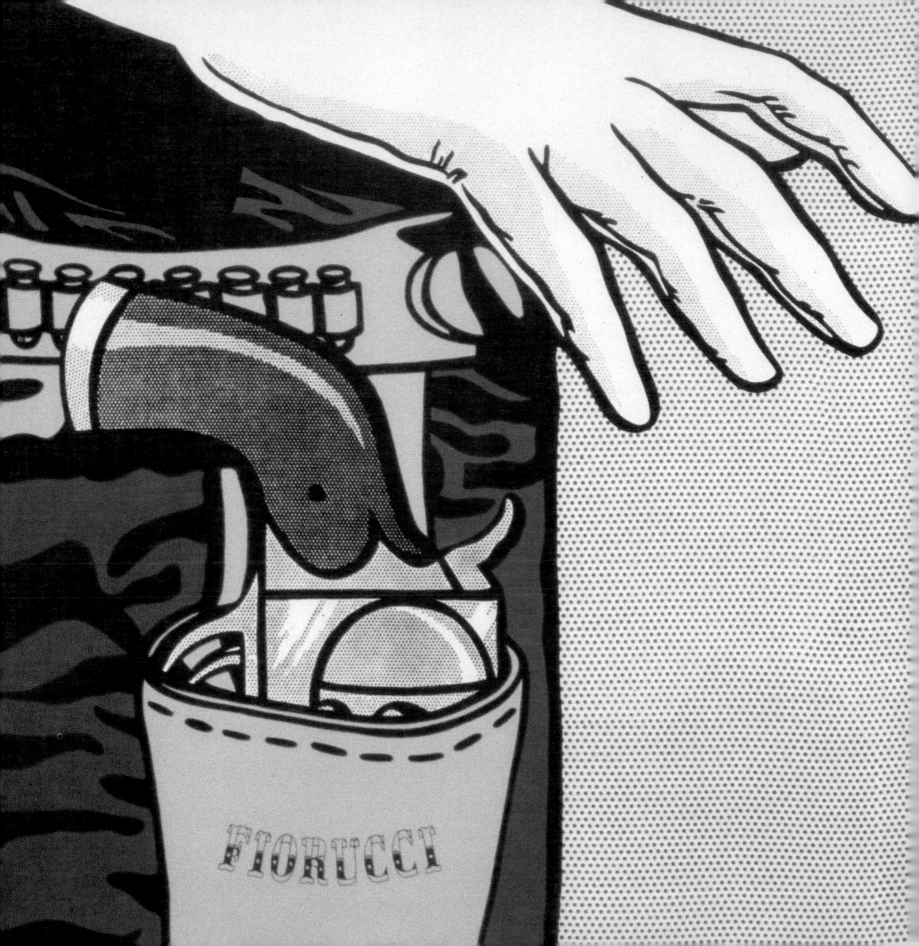

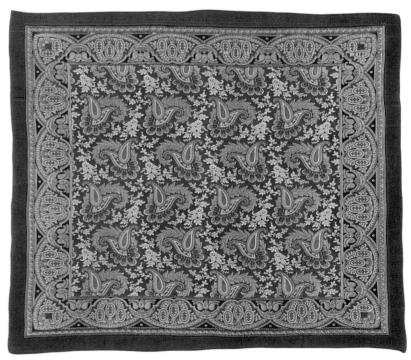

27

With Roy Rogers and Dale Evans the public saw that women could wear cowboy kerchiefs and Stetsons, and a huge licensing agreement was born. Not least of this was a 1945 "King of the Cowboys" silk scarf that featured Roy and his horse, Trigger, in lookalike horseshoe frames, the scarf bordered by a coral fence and featuring a decoratively tooled saddle in one corner and a rifle in the other. The Rogers tie-ins sold second only to Walt Disney's plethora of merchandise.

Even Howdy Doody became an important merchandising tool, his cotton kerchief an integral part of the puppet sold in toy stores. The Howdy Doody cotton handkerchief showed Howdy lassoing in a flowing white neckerchief.

In time, though, the public seemed to have its fill of Western movies and television shows, and with the passing out of favor of the cowboy stars went the promotional cowboy scarf. But the idea of the West still holds great romance—as does the neckerchief.

Not every man who wore a scarf wanted to be a cowboy. A

Patterned handkerchiefs added a touch of color and daring to the city suit. These English examples from the 1930s could be Jazz-age relatives of the cotton bandana.

Opposite: Western souvenir scarves were often poorly printed on cheap silk, unlike this surprising air-brushed and tie-died scarf.

Overleaf: Pattern and design in men's handkerchiefs became deeper and more intricate, as is evident in these details of 1930s English pieces.

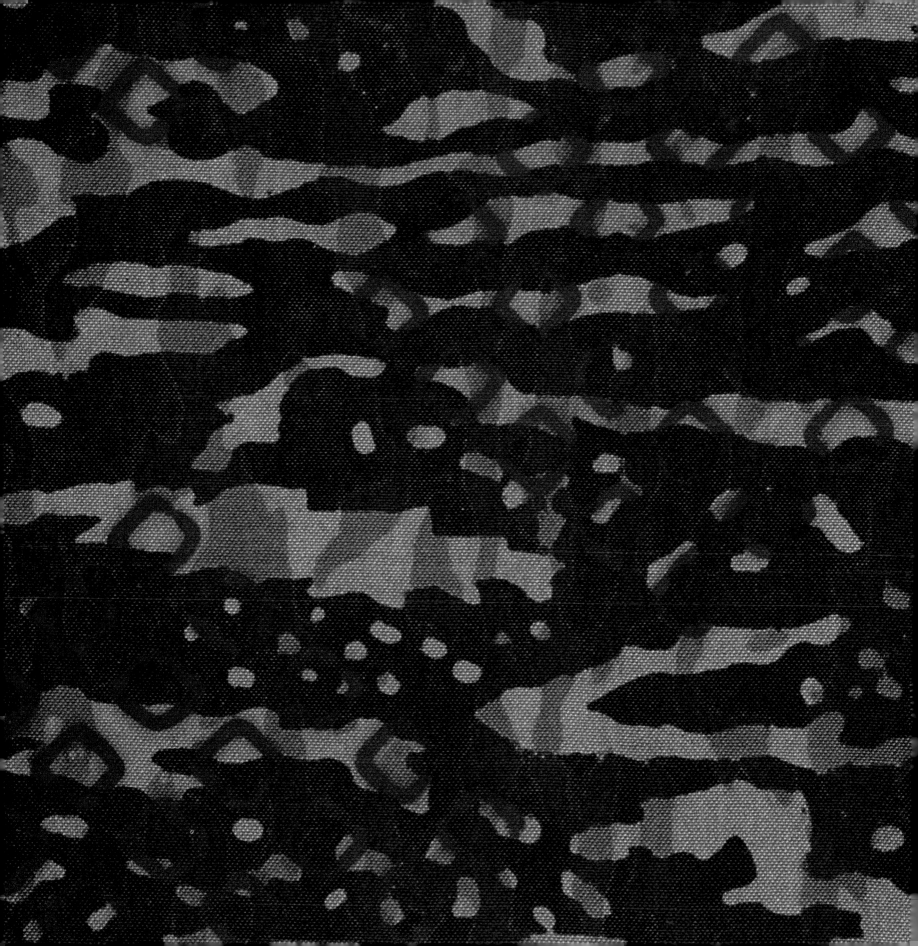

cravat—in floral silk, madras checks, or a solid color—was absolutely de rigueur *for the early nineteenth-century Romantics and dandies who followed in the wake of Beau Brummell and Byron, both advocates of the "large square of muslin, sometimes starched, knotted or tied."*

Ever since, the well-dressed man, typified in the 1920s and 1930s by the Duke of Windsor, Fred Astaire, and Noel Coward, has often tucked a restrained silk ascot or square into his open-necked shirt. In Hollywood, stars like Douglas Fairbanks, Cary Grant, or Errol

Flynn followed this tradition. There was an entire "English in Hollywood" contingent, led by C. Aubrey Smith, who organized its own cricket eleven and embraced the country-squire school of dress. William Powell, who wasn't an Englishman but sometimes dressed like one in his Thin Man *series, favored a fringed white silk scarf worn with a tuxedo, a dapper fashion on both sides of the Atlantic; Maurice Chevalier enthusiastically adopted this style, too.*

But the ascot, however casually tied, has never felt really comfortable to the average American male. Brooke Cadwallader's "Bronzini" silk squares were more popular; for example, in the 1950s, Montgomery Clift and Truman Capote often tucked them into a coat collar. The subtle, discreet colors and rich patterning of these squares added just the right touch to a conservative outfit.

Scarves and ascots became de rigeur for the well-dressed Hollywood star. *At left*, William Powell; *above*, Noel Coward and Douglas Fairbanks, Jr., in ascot; *opposite*, Cary Grant.

Stars in Scarves

To gauge the full effect of the scarf on the public consciousness, one has only to dig into the photo archives of newspapers and the libraries of photo agencies. Their files contain hundreds of news shots of stars in scarves.

Here is Audrey Hepburn, getting married to Dr. Andrea Dotti in Rome in 1969, wearing a headscarf. And over there is Elizabeth Taylor, boarding a jet alongside Mike Todd in the 1950s, looking beautiful in a voluminous dark square. Here's Liz again, wearing a headscarf as she leaves a London hospital after emergency surgery in the 1960s. And there's Marilyn Monroe, heartbreakingly tearful, announcing her divorce from Joe DiMaggio on a Beverly Hills lawn, also wearing a headscarf. The scarf in these pictures seems to be a cover-up, giving the famous actress a disguise, a hint of anonymity or mystery, just as effectively as her dark glasses.

Other pictures show Brigitte Bardot, a leopardskin-print

chiffon square just containing her tumbling beehive, and Gene Tierney leaving El Morocco in the 1940s, a Palm Beach souvenir scarf lying against her tanned shoulders. Lana Turner enlivened many of her sweater-girl pin-ups with a small scarf twisted around her throat like a necklace.

By the classical way in which she draped it, Katharine Hepburn was able to turn a white silk scarf into something approaching a commandingly regal headdress. And one can hardly find a publicity shot of the ladylike Grace Kelly in the early 1950s without a scarf spilling from her pocket or held coolly in her hand. Edith Head outdid herself in To Catch a Thief when outfitting Kelly in a very wide straw brim worn over a crisp black scarf. The scarf showed through the straw brim to form a mysterious hat. It was supposed to lure Cary

Left: Jean Harlow (c. 1930)—the scarf was not necessarily just to cover one's head.

Grant (along with a picnic lunch)—and it worked!

The 1950s were really the peak years of the scarf in the movies, since they were the years of the first popular films of Grace Kelly, Audrey Hepburn, and Marilyn Monroe, all of whom wore scarves on camera and off. In many of these films, the white scarf was used to suggest purity, or even a lid holding down the natural impulses, and indeed for much of the decade, a white silk or chiffon square was a staple in every "nice" girl's wardrobe. It was embraced by movie stars as different as Bardot in St. Tropez and Mamie Van Doren in Hollywood, and the more hair piled under the scarf, the better; the scarf could then give the impression of barely restraining a luxurious tumble of tresses.

By 1959, the scarf was being used on screen to help denote character, and nowhere is this better illustrated than in Alfred Hitchcock's Vertigo. Here Kim Novak, in Edith Head's costumes, portrays both Madeleine and Judy. Madeleine, sedate wife of a rich businessman, dresses in navy with a long gray chiffon scarf pinned high at her throat with a diamond clip. Judy, whom the lovesick James Stewart tracks down and transforms back into Madeleine, wears a blouse with the top buttons sexily undone, a long skirt cinched by a wide leather belt. The end of a patterned green scarf is tucked into the belt and trails carelessly down the side of the skirt. The trailing scarf expresses eloquently, as only Edith Head could say it, that the lady is a tramp.

In Cherie's pathetic nightclub routine in Bus Stop, Marilyn Monroe sang "That Ol' Black Magic" to a bewitched Don Murray as she flicked an emerald green chiffon scarf in a brilliant parody of an awkward, nervous, amateur "chantoose." Here, the scarf transcends its mere physical presence to become an actor's telling prop.

The scarf industry's unofficial spokeswoman must surely have been Audrey Hepburn,

The playful polka dot is a perennial favorite on scarves. *Left*, Jane Fonda (early 1960s); *below*, Katharine Hepburn, (1945).

*however. She seems to have worn
a headscarf in every one of her
films from* Roman Holiday *to*
Robin and Marian. *Off-duty
candid shots of her show her as
an habitual, and extremely
chic, scarf wearer.*

*The two Hepburns, Bardot,
Kelly, Monroe: one could almost
say these stars defined themselves through their scarves and
the way they wore them; certainly, these actresses wore no
other form of headgear, if their
glossies, or "candids," are to be
believed. The importance of the
scarf—as costume and as favored off-screen cover-up—is a
well-documented fact.*

Right: Kim Novak as Madeleine
in *Vertigo*.

Opposite: Not always a square,
the scarf could also be a long,
narrow rectangle. Joan Crawford
tied this one in a simple bow.

Overleaf: Marilyn Monroe,
with a scarf knotted once around
her neck *(page 38)*. Grace Kelly
(page 39, left) carries her scarf;
Lana Turner *(right)* knots hers
loosely, like a neckerchief.

Rosie the Riveter

"American women are learning how to put planes and tanks together, how to weld and rivet!" beamed the Woman's Home Companion of October 19, 1943. "But they're also learning how to look smart in overalls and how to be glamorous after work. They are learning to fulfill both the useful and the beautiful ideal."

Scarves took on a new role when the Second World War arrived: suddenly they were used for tying up hair and keeping it safely out of the way of heavy machinery. A vital part

of America's wartime strength was its womanpower. After Pearl Harbor, three-quarters of a million women volunteered for armament factory duty. By 1944, more than 3 million women were working alongside 6 million men on the assembly lines. Many of these factories required women to wear hair protection if they had longer hair than a man's.

"If you had long hair," remembers one ex-Rosie in Rosie the Riveter Revisited, "they made you wear this thing called the snood: they had that net in the back. I hated to wear it because I looked dopey in it. Pants were just becoming fashionable. I felt like—gee whiz—it made me look different!"

Another woman interviewed for the same book said: "I wore some kind of a cap that had a net and a bill you put your goggles on. Some women wore bandannas, but most of us ended up with our hair cut short. Your hair would slip down and you'd try to get it up and your hands were filthy with chemicals and little bits of metal."

Scarves thus became a new form of practical, everyday attire. So did "slacks": as stockings became rarer and rarer, these covered the legs sensibly and smartly. And a shoulder bag, useful for holding all sorts of supplies, completed the functional wartime fashion picture.

Left: Tied simply under the chin, the scarf became a practical accessory for the woman in a factory.

Opposite: The patriotic scarf best sums up the sentiments of the "Rosie" era. *Clockwise, from upper left,* are "Just Hello" (American, 1917); "My Country t'is of Thee" (American, 1930s); "Air Force," from Echo Scarves (American, c. 1942); and "The Minute Men," also from Echo (1942).

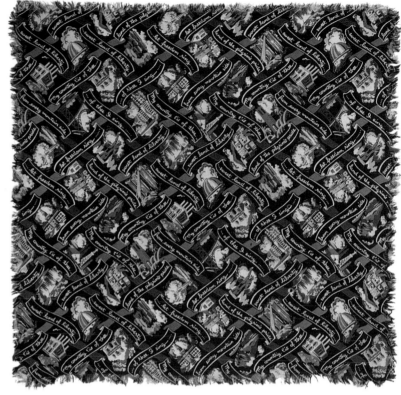

Below and opposite: The scarf tied as a turban was another signature "Rosie" look.

Right: The end of the war is commemorated here in "Unconditional Surrender" (American, 1945). The flimsy silk suggests mass-production; this scarf might have been distributed for free.

Opposite: "Forget Me Not" (American, 1917). Hopeful mothers and girlfriends held treasured keepsakes in this hankie receptacle from the First World War.

Forget
Me Not
O East or West,
its home thats best,
The saying's surely true.
For when my thoughts
would seek their rest,
They all come home-to you.
USA

Commemoratives

Just about every event in this century you can name—from the opening of a Broadway show to a world's fair, from the anniversary of a store, a street, a town, a state to the abdication of a king or the coronation of a queen—has been marked by its own special commemorative scarf. World's fair souvenir collectors, who regard the fairs held in New York and San Francisco in the 1930s as the most stylish, do not feel their collections are complete without a couple of the vivid silk scarves or handkerchiefs that marked these events. Indeed, there is a whole school of collectors interested only in this type of scarf, and some of the rarest commemoratives can be found in far-from-glamorous military and political collections.

Most scarf firms, including Jacqmar in Britain and Hermès in France, designed a square for the coronation of Queen Elizabeth II in 1953. Hermès' coronation scarf was perhaps remembered in the

1970s, when the Queen permitted a photograph of herself, wearing an Hermès scarf, to be used on Britain's 17-pence postage stamp. Now Hermès celebrates special events at the drop of a scarf—for example, its "Flora and Fauna of Texas" scarf, featuring an enormous turkey, for the Texas Sesquicentennial in 1986 and its carré for New York's Statue of Liberty Centennial in the same year.

One of the strangest commemoratives must surely be one that immortalized abdication of King Edward VIII, whose speech explaining his renunciation of his throne and kingdom "for the woman I love" was reprinted in sober black and white on a silk square.

Above left: "Esposizione Universale," the fascist World's Fair (Italian, 1942). *Above:* In "We Shall Never Surrender," Winston Churchill—himself an avid collector of scarves—is shown amid snippets from his speeches (British, c. 1943).

Opposite: Even the days of the week were commemorated, as shown in this collection of American calendar scarves.

Overleaf: Lilly Daché designed this clever convention souvenir for pharmacists' wives to use as a guide (American, c. 1955). *Page 47, clockwise from top left:* "Vive France Libre" (French, 1942); "Golden Gate International Exposition," San Francisco, California (American, 1939); "New York World's Fair 1939," one of the many colorfully designed examples, much sought after by collectors; and a 1986 reissue of Echo's "S.S. Nieuw Amsterdam" (American, c. 1950).

VIVE FRANCE LIBRE

JEANNE D'ARC — LIBÉRATRICE DE LA FRANCE
ARRIVE EST LE TRIOMPHE
POUR LA VICTOIRE — ARC DE TRIOMPHE
ALLONS ENFANTS — LIBERTÉ
HONNEUR ET PATRIE
VIVE — DE GAULLE
CATHÉDRALE DE STRASBOURG
EGALITÉ — DE LA PATRIE — FRATERNITÉ — LE JOUR
DE GLOIRE

TREASURE ISLE
SAN FRANCISCO GOLDEN GATE INTERNATIONAL WORLDS FAIR
1939

HOLLAND AMERICA LINE

VIENNA — BERLIN — LEIPSIC
CHICAGO — BOSTON — ST LOUIS
NEW YORK   NEW YORK
BRÜNN — INNSBRUCK
PARIS — GENEVA

s.s. Nieuw Amsterdam
36287 TONS

ROTTERDAM AMSTERDAM

World Fair 1939

Great Britain — Argentine — Brazil — Peru — Venezuela

Brooke Cadwallader

A document from the vaults of the Metropolitan Museum of Art Costume Institute, dated 1951 and written by fashion publicist Eleanor Lambert, credits Brooke Cadwallader—the first "name" designer of American fashion-label scarves—with making the scarf "an article of American fashion."

Reputed never to have put pen to paper, Cadwallader evidently masterminded his team of artists from a New York atelier at the corner of Canal Street and Broadway. His editions of scarves were strictly limited, printed by hand on the finest materials.

His limited-edition scarves read, "This print signed by the artist is number __" with the number handwritten in. Sometimes the Cadwallader crest was printed alongside. The "Number One" scarf of each year's special edition was sent to the current First Lady at the White House.

Cadwallader prints depict a

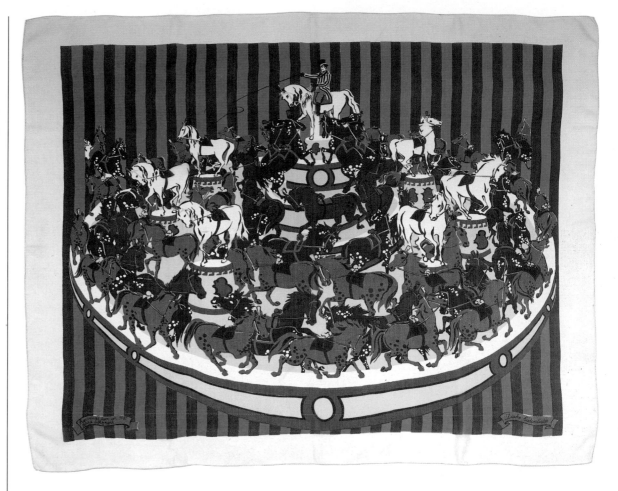

variety of historical subjects that usually teach you something: "Explorers"; "Musical Instruments"; "Victorian Silhouettes"; "Beau Brummell"; and "Maps and Measuring Devices" are precise, deadpan renderings of past ages or historical facts. Clean, uncluttered, no-

nonsense, and crisp, they prefigure the space-filled look of 1950s American graphic art.

In 1950, ill health forced Cadwallader to retire to Mexico, where he continued to manufacture his scarves. He died late in the decade.

At the time, Cadwallader was the only American rival to Hermès. *Above:* "Circus Poster" (c. 1949). *Opposite, from top:* "Declaration of Independence" (1950), "Ostriches and Oranges" (c. 1952), "Midsummer Fantasy" (this was originally designed by Joan Lang for Hattie Carnegie), "Early Automobiles" (early 1950s). Among the scarves shown with the model is "Declaration of Independence."

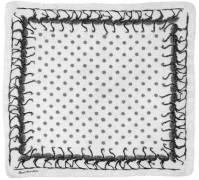

49

Hermès

What do you get if you cross a horse with a silk scarf? An Hermès carré! Instantly identifiable by its bits, straps, buckles, ribbons, medallions, and kit and tack, an Hermès carré (you never call it a scarf) confers instant status upon its wearer. Nowhere is the magic of the scarf more potent than in this high-quality passport to "carré society," worn by everyone from the Queen of England on down. And Hermès knows it! A recent editorial in its sumptuous catalogue stated, "The golden rule of French stores is that the customer is king. . . . Hermès is no exception, the subtle difference being that Hermès' customers are literally kings!"

Hermès, founded as a harness-maker's in 1837, hit pay dirt when it began printing its own scarves 100 years later. Now silk squares and ties account for more than half its revenues, but their horsey look reflects the company's origins. Even now its equestrian mu-

seum in Paris is an important source for Hermès' designers. When they depart from the equine theme, they turn to other motifs that evoke the aristocratic life: coats of arms, banners, epaulettes, tassels.

In America, black, navy, and red carrés sell best, the classic sellers usually depicting horsey themes: "Brides de Gala"; "Ex Libris"; "Apron d'Or"; "Springs"; "Voiture de Transformation." Most often reprinted are "Les Clefs," "Napoleon," "Regina," and "Promenade de Longchamps." A flagship store usually stocks a

range of up to 120 patterns. Some women get so hooked that they attempt to track down all 820 designs produced since 1937! They comb used-clothing stores, antique dealers, and advertisements to locate the scarves they are missing.

Hermès credits its emphasis on quality for its success. The firm is now believed to offer the best silk scarves on the market, and, since more people can afford the best scarf than the best car or yacht, they sell in large quantities. However, an Hermès is not the most expensive scarf one can buy. As of this

Far left: "Eperons d'Or" (1974); *left:* "Promenade de Longchamps" (1970)—twenty-five screens were used to achieve the depth and richness of color; *below:* As lapels, "Mors à la connétable" (1970), as belt, "Cuivreries" (1985).

Opposite, clockwise from top left: "Les Perroquets" (1986), "Eperons d'Or" (1974); "Equateur" (1988), and "Sangles" (1984).

writing, it costs $175 in the United States, whereas other makes can sell for as much as $250, depending on the size and artist.

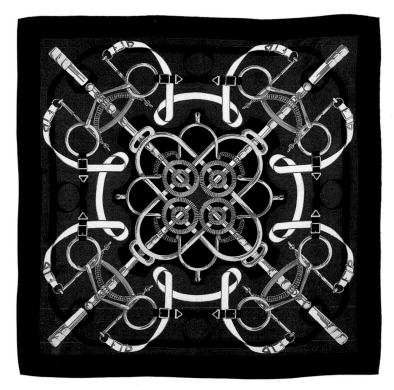

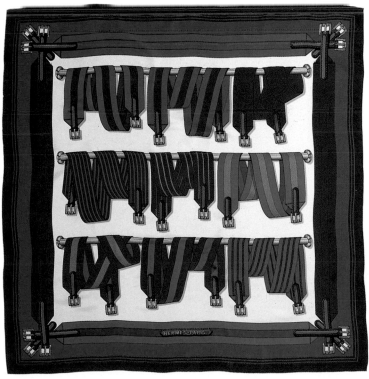

Opposite, clockwise from top left: the 150th Anniversary Commemorative scarves, "Feux d'Artifice" (1987); "Queen," created in honor of the coronation of Queen Elizabeth II (1952); "Napoléon," one of Hermès' most popular and enduring designs (1963); "Liberty," commemorating the centennial of the Statue of Liberty (1986).

Below: Part of a line of ready-to-wear clothing created with scarf material; here, "Tourbillons" is used for a suit.

Hermès weaves its silk en bias after intertwining nine fibers in a single strand, producing a finer, more durable silk that holds its shape extraordinarily well. The firm proudly claims that it takes up to nine or even twelve months to produce a new scarf, using up to forty-five screens to break down the colors. Great care is taken to trace and place the patterns so that each color exactly tallies. Each scarf is printed on a 100-yard-long table, where the lengths of Chinese silk twill are attached. Once the colors have been applied, they are steam-fixed, and the silk is washed to remove silkworm residues. The scarf is then roller-squeezed, air-dried, and sized. The hem is hand-rolled inward, and Hermès advises ironing only on the reverse side and never pressing the edge, so the hem always retains its distinctive look.

Today, Hermès' catalogues are thick, glossy affairs that advertise the firm's clothing, scarves, and luggage. The clothing is classic, extremely expensive, and often lined in, or made of, Hermès' own silk squares. The luggage is so beautiful that one would fear for its life on any baggage carrousel. But the scarves still rule the roost. Like Rolls-Royce, Hermès is an ultimate brand name, and it is no coincidence that Rolls-Royce advertises in Hermès' catalogues.

Above: A partial view of the Hermès printing room, where a staff of 160 apply color after color to the scarves. Depending on the complexity of the design, up to thirty-five colors may be hand silk-screened.

Overleaf: A detail of "Napoléon."

LEDOUX

Vera

No one in scarf design has been as prolific—or as sensible—as Vera. Born in 1907 and still putting in a full day's work at her Croton-on-Hudson studio eighty years later, Vera Neumann is chairwoman of the world's largest scarf-manufacturing company. Her signature scarves are credited as being the first "designer scarves" designed by an American; certainly they were the first to sport a female textile designer's signature.

Graduating from Cooper Union in New York, she started the firm of Vera with her husband, George Neumann, in 1945. After buying some surplus parachute silk from the U.S. government, George Neumann suggested that his young wife design a few scarves for it. Her

first scarf, designed in 1947, depicted ferns, flowers, and herbs and sold for $5. Collectors of vintage Vera say that the smaller the signature on the scarf, the earlier the design.

In the 1950s, Vera introduced the clashing shades of orange, pink, lime green, and yellow. Her inspiration has usually come from nature, the fine arts, and her frequent travels to Europe and the Orient. Backed by a design team of fifteen, Vera produces more than 500 designs annually for her three different scarf collections.

In addition to her well-known sketchy, almost cartoony, animals, ladybugs (her personal trademark), and flowers, Vera's style embraces geometrics, folk art, and sophisticated patterns and abstracts. Each design is translated into a black-and-white version, as the firm feels that these are steady sellers. Vera is very careful about copyrighting her designs and renewing this copyright if a pattern is to be reissued.

Vera's greatest talent may be

her ability to take the most outrageous contemporary designs, apply to them her sane, clean-cut taste, and produce an acceptable product for the woman who is not interested in making a fashion statement or being a fashion victim. She has, however, gone off on some surprising design binges, especially during the 1960s, when her startling color combinations rivaled those of Pucci and Peter Max.

These scarves depict various stages in Vera's prolific design history. *Above:* "Floral" (late 1960s). *Left:* "Patchwork" (mid-1950s). *Opposite:* A detail of "Abstract" (early 1950s).

Echo

Founded in 1923 by Edgar C. Hyman (his initials form the first three letters of the firm's name), Echo has remained a family business and one of America's oldest and largest scarf and accessory manufacturers, second only to Vera. Echo also markets the Ralph Lauren "Polo" scarf collections for men and women. Its current president, Dorothy Roberts, is Edgar Hyman's daughter.

Echo's "Signature" collection is its most fashionable, using silk, crepe, satin, and wool for designs printed in up to eighteen colors. Details like hand-braided fringe, hand-beading, and sequining enliven "Signature" scarves, which also feature paisleys, metallics, and ethnic patterns. Aiming at Middle America, and with 4,000 retailers selling its goods, Echo indeed echoes current trends, colors, and styles.

Above: "See Red," an advertisement for Max Factor lipstick (late 1960s). *Left:* "Persian Garden" (1955). *Far left and opposite:* "Floral" (late 1950s).

Tammis Keefe

Born in San Francisco in 1920, Tammis Keefe is now a cult name among scarf collectors. She began designing for the scarf firm of Kimbal in 1953, and, during her tragically short life—she died at the age of forty in 1960—Keefe was extremely prolific. Unlike Cadwallader, she designed and painted each scarf herself. She was the first woman after Vera to sign her name to her scarves. Her muted colors and whimsical, almost cartoony, style are more obviously commercial than Cadwallader's. They perfectly typify the innocent, carefree mood of the early 1950s.

Keefe's trips to Europe and Asia inspired much of her work. A visit to Italy was reflected in a commedia dell'arte scarf, and India influenced her delightful design of turbaned, polo-playing maharajahs surrounded by a leopardskin border.

Above: "Cats" (mid-1950s).

Opposite: "21 Club, no. 4" (early 1950s). Keefe also created the no. 3 scarf for the "21 Club."

Liberty

Arthur Lasenby Liberty opened his London store in 1875 after an apprenticeship at Farmer and Rogers' Great Shawl and Cloak Emporium. With the rise of the Aesthetic movement, London was ready for his imported shawls and Indian silks, and he rode the crest of the wave of these Oriental textiles' popularity. Liberty fabrics' natural dyes, called "art colors," offered a soothing, superior alternative to the brash synthetic hues of mass-produced goods. Liberty's hand-blocked silks were bought by private dressmakers and made up into "artistic" dresses.

In 1904, Liberty began manufacturing goods under its own label, having acquired Littler's block-printing works. Handkerchiefs, scarves, and other items were produced, making Liberty's the Laura Ashley of its day, known for traditional floral patterns and exotic imported paisleys.

During the 1920s, Liberty's designed a scarf every year for the famous Derby horse race. Printed before the race, the scarf awaited only the name of the winner, which was rushed to the printers on horseback so that the completed square could be sold to the crowds returning from Epsom Downs.

In the 1930s and 1940s, Liberty's specialities included colorful silks, printed linens, cretonnes and fine wools, men's

Above: "Ianthe." First used for a scarf in 1982, this pattern was originally designed in the 1890s.

Left: A Tena Lawn floral (1985), inspired by Egyptian cotton florals of the 1920s.

ties and dressing gowns. In the late 1950s, a revival of interest in Art Nouveau prompted Liberty's to reprint, using silk-screen, its swirling, sinuous, turn-of-the-century designs on silk foulard, chiffon, wool, and organza. The store also launched a full-scale promotion of the "Liberty Look" in America.

Liberty's has never tried to go modern, although the 1960s' vogue for Indian music and gurus, paisleys, and exotica swept it into the "Swinging London" scene. Its later "Jazz Age," "Tango," and "Landscape" lines were all reflected in its silk headsquares. Today, Liberty's is thought of as traditional, classic, and still scarf-conscious, and in 1987 it hosted "The Scarf Show," an exhibit of 400 vintage scarves.

Above: "Bauhaus" (1969), adapted by Susan Collier from an original Liberty tapestry.

Left: a 1985 abstract.

Overleaf: A detail of "Hera" (1974). The pattern was originally designed in 1887 by Arthur Silver.

Walking Billboards

In the late 1940s, manufacturers quickly realized the scarf's promotional potential. They saw that if they distributed a scarf with the name of a firm, a perfume, or a movie emblazoned across it, then every time it was worn it would represent free advertising. The heads of fashionable women sitting on buses, eating at restaurants, going to the races—and promoting the names Chanel, Dior, Hermès—repaid the cost of the scarf many times over.

Show business capitalized on this trend in a big way: souvenir scarves of Broadway hits like South Pacific, Guys and Dolls, Brigadoon, and Finian's Rainbow were made and sold, and the tradition survives with scarves advertising Les Misérables and Phantom of the Opera.

A L'il Abner silk square in nine colors was launched in

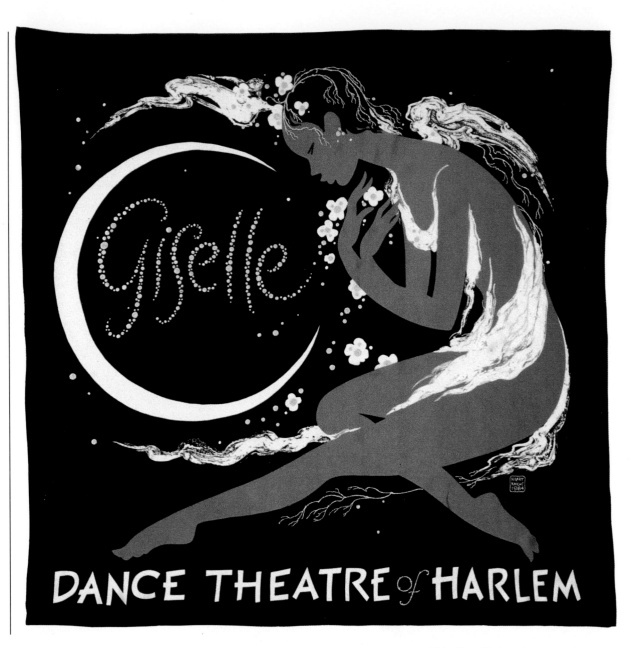

"Giselle," designed in 1984 by Hilary Knight for New York's Dance Theatre of Harlem.

1949 with nationwide television and radio advertising. Retailing at $1.98, it featured Daisy Mae, the Dogpatch Gang, and the Schmoos, alongside Abner. Even today, the promotional scarf takes in all the latest crazes: a rather pricey Roger Rabbit silk square celebrated the 1988 hit movie, for example.

Promotional scarves were produced for the movie Gone With the Wind. A Shirley Temple scarf was issued in the 1930s, a Beatles scarf followed in the 1960s, a host of scarves promoting other singers, film stars, and movies were made as well.

Some scarf collectors concentrate on this category, as it offers a particular challenge: promotional scarves are usually produced in small quantities and often disappear without a trace.

Above: "Les Surprises de Fath," by couturier Jacques Fath (French, early 1950s).

Overleaf, clockwise from top left: Al Capp's "Dogpatch" (American, 1948) originally sold for $1.98; "Fashion Magazines" (English, c. 1958); the "Harper's Bazaar" Christmas gift (American, 1980); "Jessica Rabbit," designed by Wendy Gell (American, 1988); "Bugs Bunny" (American, 1940s); "Derby Winners" (English, 1959); "Gay Times at Churchills Club," designed by Arthur Ferrier (English, 1950s); and "Charlie Chaplin" (1930s).

The "21" Christmas Gift

The mystique of "21 Club" scarves lay in the fact that you couldn't buy them; they had to be given you. No wonder everyone wanted one and that today they are among the hardest scarves to collect.

The "21 Club" was never a club, although its guests often treated it as one. It originated as a somewhat shady Greenwich Village speakeasy in the 1920s. The legend goes that Jack Kriendler and Charlie Berns, the proprietors, gave everyone such a warm welcome that by the time they moved their establishment uptown, "Jack and Charlie's 21" was the place to be seen. It became a New York institution, frequented by such celebrities as Aristotle Onassis, the Duke and Duchess of Windsor, Marlene Dietrich, Ingrid Bergman, Lillian Hellman, Elsa Maxwell, Bea Lillie, and several American presidents and their families.

In the early 1950s, the restaurant began the custom of making up its own silk scarves and giving them to female guests at Christmas. These became so popular that men clamored for theirs, and matching pocket squares were introduced some time later.

Each year, a design was made up in four different colorways. The scarves were usually square, although for three years a long, 6- by 1-foot scarf was produced. They provide a potted history of scarf design between the 1950s and the 1970s. Each featured the restaurant's jockey symbol and the pattern of its decorative iron railings at 21 West 52nd Street. Tammis Keefe designed two of the first year's gifts (nos. 3 and 4; all scarves were numbered); no. 10 was based on the restaurant's mural by Charles Baskerville. The prettiest was no. 16, a multicolored mosaic that, on close inspection, turns out to be a jockey. Ray Strauss did some of

the 1960s designs, whose neon colors reflected the psychedelia of that time. The restaurant amassed its own little hoard of art by Frederic Remington, and the very last "21" scarf featured his bronco rider. The scarves were discontinued in the early 1970s, to everyone's regret, and the "21 Club" passed out of the Kriendler family's hands in 1986.

Above: No. 18 (1960s); *opposite:* No. 16 (1960s).

Overleaf: Scarves from the 1950s and 60s, featuring nos. 6, 12, 15, 22, and 23.

Wish You Were Here

In the late 1940s and early 1950s, as peace and prosperity returned after the Depression and the Second World War, travel and vacationing boomed. Tourists had always bought and sent postcards or had themselves photographed in front of an important monument to prove that they had traveled. Then some clever individual thought up the souvenir travel scarf, which did the same thing in a more fashionable way. It was really like wearing a fabric postcard on your head, and it did not always entail going too far from home. Of course, a souvenir scarf from Hawaii perhaps had more cachet than one from Palm Springs or San Francisco. And a scarf from Paris or London proclaimed its wearer to be a true jet setter.

Throughout the 1950s, as more and more Americans discovered the rest of the world, the travel scarf came into its own,

becoming the first calling card of the Great American Tourist! A little on the lurid side, sometimes downright gaudy, travel scarves were always cheerful, often relentlessly so, usually showing views, local color, and perhaps a slogan or two.

Above: Two scarves with travel themes. "Visa" shows various luggage labels from around the world; "Bon Voyage" depicts luggage ready to be boarded on a cruise ship.

Opposite: "Fiesta" (American, 1950s)—bright South American colors fill this charming scarf.

When in Paris, one shops for scarves (see above, lower left corner), then wears them. The travel scarf can often serve as a record of lost times. "New York" commemorates one of the high points of 1930s movie-going: The Roxy Theatre. The "Chicago" airport of the 1940s bears little resemblance to the sprawl of today's O'Hare.

Left: A complete view of "Bon Voyage" (see page 74). *Below, far left:* The breezy "Home Lines" (Italian, 1955) is a tribute to sea travel. *Below, left:* "Exotic Dancer" (American, 1950s) conjures up a land that is not quite real.

Opposite: Noted fashion model Lisa captures the free spirit of travel in this photo.

Fight, Team, Fight!

Although many Americans were traveling in the 1950s, not everyone had the wherewithal to become a jet setter. Nevertheless, most people could still get out to a ball game. Scarf manufacturers caught on, and during the late 1940s and early 1950s, the "sport" scarf put in an appearance.

Like travel scarves, sport scarves could be a bit flashy—the colors could be strong for some tastes—and there was a scarf for just about every sport. Football scarves may have been the most popular, but skiing, golf, fishing, horseback riding, and even roller skating were all represented on silk. A July 1949 Neiman Marcus scarf advertisement, aimed at college girls, suggested, "Carry the football schedule around in your head: wear the Neiman Marcus South West Conference Scarf!" At $4.95, it wasn't high fashion, but this wearable calendar could be a great way to impress your boyfriend.

Below, left to right: "Ski Angel" (American, late 1940s); "Football Date Sheet," a functional gimmick scarf (American, 1937); "Roller Derby" (American, 1950s).

Bottom: A detail of "High School Football." The young woman at left sports a well-tied scarf.

"Men at Play," a Carol Stanley
scarf by Dorothy Liebes
(American, late 1950s).

True Romance

There are women who claim that the most romantic gesture a man can make is to present them with an article of clothing, carefully chosen, that reflects their mutual taste. A scarf is probably the most popular and easily accessible garment to be given in this manner, perhaps recalling the medieval practice of ladies lending handkerchiefs to knights for good luck and for a romantic incentive to excel in combat.

Left: Dior's "Roses sur Paris" (French, mid-1950s).

Below: Elizabeth Taylor and Laurence Harvey in *Butterfield 8* (1960).

Overleaf, clockwise from top left: "The Big Apple" (1930s), "Record Hopping" (1950s), "Tango" (1950s), and "Cherchez la Femme" (1950s)—all are American, all depict classic themes in romantic scarves.

Along with flowers and chocolates, a silk scarf is probably one of the best-selling romantic gifts. Sometimes, it must be admitted, the romantic scarf can be every bit as saccharine as a chocolate box. During the 1950s, for instance, a scarf almost had to be illustrated with a few nonchalantly scattered roses. Ballerinas were also a big 1950s motif, perhaps due to the popularity of the film The Red Shoes. But the romance of scarves dates back to when the way you wore your scarf was a way of communicating who you were. In sixteenth-century Europe, it was said that

the way a woman knotted or draped her kerchief could reveal the very village from which she hailed. This "secret language" of scarves has largely survived into the present.

In India, the loose part of a sari, which is actually a very long scarf entwined around the body, is used to hide behind or peer from. Similarly, an Arab veil, or yashmak, can be used for modesty and/or for flirting, according to the mood and morals of the wearer.

No such mixed messages clouded the wearing of "romance" scarves in 1950s America. Men were home from the wars, and dating became a popular national pastime. Romance magazines like True Story and True Confessions were all the rage, as were fan magazines highlighting "ideal" couples like Eddie and Debbie, Tony and Janet. The mushy, gushy visual endearments of True Love comics were reproduced—ad nauseam, but often very amusingly—on scarves. This theme was re-

prised in the 1960s, when artists like Roy Lichtenstein used the romance comic as a source for his paintings, and shops like Fiorucci adopted it for their scarves.

The romance of vintage scarves, which evolved in the 1960s, reflects the nostalgia of wearing clothes from a bygone era, imagining who wore them

before you, and slipping back in time, always a romantic pursuit, to escape the harsh realities of today's world. Throwing a silky vintage scarf over your head, you can be transported to a soda shop for a fun date, or off to Paris to view the collections, a wicked 1920s vamp, or Audrey Hepburn in Funny Face, according to your mood, while an Hermès carré from the 1950s instantly sweeps you into the jet-set world of horse-racing and travel and is probably the only garment you have in common with European royalty.

Far left: Audrey Hepburn in *Breakfast at Tiffany's* (1961).

Left: "Hearts 'n Keys" (American, mid-1950s).

Opposite, clockwise from top left: Another Lichtenstein-inspired Fiorucci scarf (Italian, c. 1975); "Friday Night Date" (American, mid-1950s); "Talk, Talk, Talk" (American, late 1950s); and "Champagne and Dreams" (American, early 1950s).

Born in Florence in 1914 to one of Italy's oldest, noblest families, the Marchese Pucci Barsento, more popularly known as Emilio Pucci, started as a dilettante designer in a tiny resort boutique on the island of Capri in the early 1950s and parlayed his talent and color sense into a world-famous empire. His admirers have sometimes credited him with being as influential as Coco Chanel. Certainly, in the 1960s, Pucci's prints were everywhere, worn by the world's most famous, most beautiful women, including Elizabeth Taylor, Marilyn Monroe, and Jacqueline Kennedy.

Pucci's first designs were inspired by his underwater photography. He took his color photographs to a Como textile manufacturer and asked for silks that reproduced the aquamarine, turquoise, emerald, and coral hues of the Mediterranean waters. He was told that it would be impossible to render these brilliant colors on silk, but he persevered until a workable process was developed.

The bright colors first shocked, then intrigued, his clients. "Postwar fashion was hungry for color," Stanley Marcus has explained. Pucci's scarf designs were so innovative that he was an easy victim of what New York's garment trade calls "knock-off artists." To guarantee that his devotees would get a true-blue Pucci print (his imitators produced almost-identical copies), he was advised to sign his name on every yard of silk he printed. Today, this is the collector's guide to the real thing. However, since he is of noble lineage, Pucci felt he could not use his family name, so the signature reads "Emilio."

It is a chicken-and-egg question as to whether Pucci influenced his contemporaries or they him. Nor is it clear whether he is actually an artist himself. He has been known to stand behind artists, demanding, correcting, and cajoling to get exactly the look he wants. But whatever one thinks of this somewhat overbearing personage, he has conferred his own special magic onto everything he has designed, from stewardesses' outfits for Braniff to logos for the U.S. space program.

Pucci continues to turn out his happy, colorful patterns, which waft us right back to the heady days of the 1960s and which are starting to look strangely right again as the 1990s approach.

Three scarves from the 1960s by Emilio Pucci.

Suitable for Framing

In 1947, as part of his introduction to a catalogue of an exhibit of silk scarves designed by some of the world's greatest artists, the English art expert Sacheverell Sitwell wrote: "A scarf is a mere square of silk intended to be worn around the head. But it can be treated as a work of art. It can be collected like a rare book or print."

Since the beginning of the century, fine artists have been attracted to designing on a square of silk. Perhaps they like the idea of their colors becoming transparent; possibly they enjoy the thought of their creation being worn by a beautiful woman instead of being framed and hung on a museum wall. . . .

Bernard Buffet signed his name to several scarves in the 1950s; his dramatic, black-and-white spiky lines admirably suited a headsquare. One of his best is a painting of bookshelves, printed in 1959 by René

Juillard, a French publisher, as a Christmas gift for his employees. Saul Steinberg was published in silk by Piazza Fabrics, circa 1960.

But perhaps the zenith of the art scarf was reached by Zika Ascher, a Hungarian textile manufacturer with highbrow tastes who set up business in London in 1939. He began by making unusual, high-quality fabrics—silks, wools, tweeds—in an effort to sustain a high-

One-of-a-kind scarves created in 1988. *Left:* Michael Longacre; *above:* Paul Davis. *Opposite, bottom row:* Bill E. Sullivan, Koos van den Akker, Hilary Knight, James McMullan, Milton Glaser; *second row:* David Sandlin, Janet Fish, Kenny Scharf, David Lance Goines, Al Harp, Ronnie Cutrone, Patricia Pastor for Perry Ellis; *third row:* Rodney Alan Greenblat, Paul Smith, Paul Davis, April Gornik, Michael Longacre, Stephen Sprouse, Nell Blaine, Nancy Hagin, Meredith McNeal; *top row:* Maurice Sendak, Hubert de Givenchy, David Byrd/Joe Bessera, Marcy Katcher.

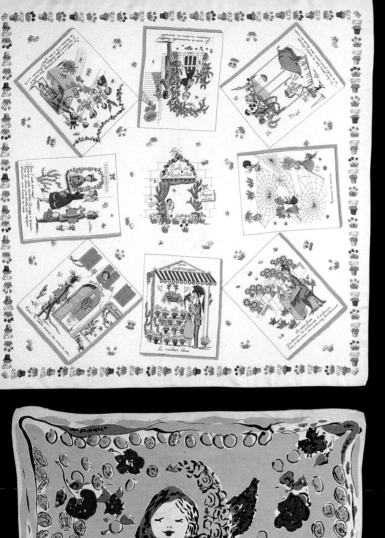

Preceding pages, clockwise from top left: Paul Cezanne, "Le Vase Bleu" (American, early 1950s); a Piero Fornasetti scarf (Italian, 1950s); Peynet's "Ecole des Fleuristes" (French, 1950s); James Thurber's "Thurber Dogs" (American, 1953) was commissioned by Richard Farrar and originally sold for $2.98; "Still Life," by Bernard Buffet (French, c. 1959); Vertès' "Angel of Prosperity" (American, late 1940s); a 1987 reissue of a 1946 Zika Ascher scarf, Henry Moore's "Standing Figures"; a 1987 reissue of Jean Cocteau's "Visage," originally sold by Ascher in 1947 for $30.00.

Above: "Sketch Pad" (European, 1940s).

fashion company that would attract only the very top designers as clients. Then, in 1947, Ascher commissioned Henri Matisse, Henry Moore, Jean Cocteau, André Derain, and others to add status, prestige, and good taste to his firm and, incidentally, to raise the status of the humble scarf. Retailing at the then very high prices of $12 to $48 (priced according to the fame of the artist), the scarves were exhibited throughout the world as if they were paintings—stretched, framed, and lit.

Perhaps Ascher was ahead of his time, or perhaps women did not yet have the necessary funds for what was still a luxury item. Whatever the reasons, the scarves did not fare well. However, the notion of the scarf as art attracted a lot of attention. Excited by the involvement of leading artists, the art critics flocked to this fashion collection and reviewed it as they would an art exhibit. In doing so, they raised the very interesting issues of what exactly makes a scarf, what the raison d'être of scarf design is.

"Matisse and Henry Moore had the function of the scarf in mind," approved Harper's magazine. "Their scarves are designed to fold, to throw on the table, to carry crumpled in the hand, to look handsome in use, not just in a frame."

British artist Keith Vaughan wrote about his commission: "The problem is not so much to get a design which looks right in the rigid square but a design which will hold together when the square becomes fluid, the material draped." The French artist Christian Bérard, who later went on to design scarves for Dior, made his poetic comment: "Squares and scarves by Ascher have a special life of their own. They move and dance according to the gestures of the women who wear them. . . ."

The most expensive of the Ascher scarves, Matisse's "Echarpe No. 2," was limited to 275 copies and showed four beautiful stylized leaves on a pure blue background. It cost $48. John Tunnard's lavender and yellow "Bird and Stone" was limited to 225 and sold for $28. "Combat de Coqs" by Antonio Clave showed two bantams fighting it out and was limited to 672, selling for $32.

The fascination for signed artists' scarves persisted. In 1968, when photographer Bert Stern opened his store "On First" at 1159 First Avenue in New York City, he attempted to mass-market fine art by selling Roy Lichtenstein wallpaper and holding art "happenings" like James Lee Byar's "Shirt for 100 People." Sven Lukin's official "On First" scarf was a large square of huge letters printed on chiffon. Gerald Laing did a parachute scarf, and Stern himself silkscreened a portrait of Marilyn Monroe that showed the star holding up a transparent chiffon scarf to her nude body, veiling her face, a "scarf within a scarf" that made for a very arresting image.

More recently, in 1988, the leather-goods firm of Louis Vuitton climbed aboard the scarf bandwagon by commissioning artists including James Rosenquist and Sandro Chia to design scarves. And an exciting group of artists, illustrators, graphic and scenic designers, and couturiers created one-of-a-kind scarves especially for this book. Created with the understanding that they would be auctioned—the proceeds donated to the fight against AIDS—the scarves range from delightful depictions of familiar characters to vibrant paintings on silk to designs that redefine the very boundaries of what a scarf can be.

Two scarves by Bert Stern, both c. 1967. *Top:* "Marilyn I"; *bottom:* "Marilyn II."

Overleaf: A detail of Kovarsky's "Rear Window" (American, mid-1950s), commissioned by Richard Farrar.

Farrar by Kovarsky

   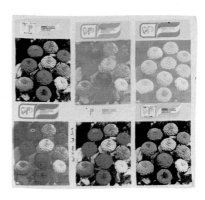

More one-of-a-kind 1988 scarves. *Top to bottom, left:* Betsey Johnson, Carmello Pomodoro, William Ivey Long, David Sandlin; *second row:* Michael Katz, Nell Blaine; *third row:* Michael Katz, Janet Fish; *right:* Paul Smith, Lane Smith, Bill Sullivan, Lois Dodd.

Overleaf: Hand-painted scarves created by Maurice Sendak, *left,* and Bill E. Sullivan, *right.*

Pages 100-101, clockwise from top left: originals by Carolina Herrera, Mary McFadden, Meredith McNeal, Oscar de la Renta, David Montgomery, Annie Kelly, Roz Chast (detail), and Lynda Benglis.

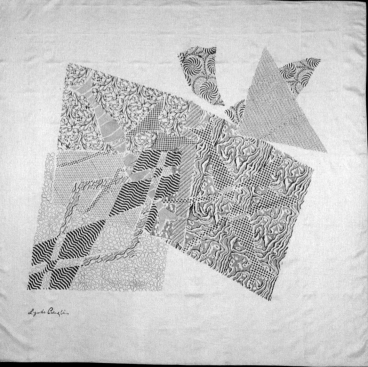

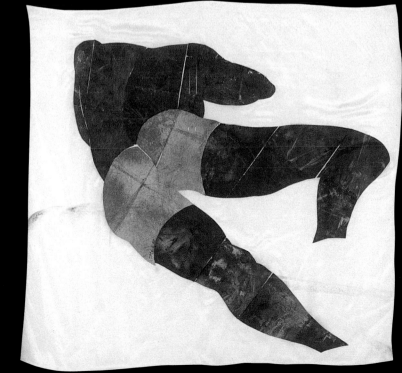

Wearable Art

"There are as many ways to wear scarves as there are scarves," announced Harper's Bazaar in 1923. The scarf may have begun as a garment without definite rules for its use, but the fashion press quickly invented some. Even today, there is no shortage of magazine articles or little booklets (many put out by scarf firms) that teach women "fifty-one different ways to tie your scarf," but the most fascinating aspect of scarves is that they allow the wearer to be creative. Ways of wearing scarves come in and out of fashion; the scarf has been wound around the neck, the forehead, the skull, the waist, trailed from the shoulder, tied on the chin, or not worn at all but simply tied nonchalantly to one's purse.

Anthropologists have called the wearing of silk a hieratic phenomenon; in other words, it represents a wish to outshine others. And certainly while there are those who have achieved fame and have also been noted for wearing scarves, it is de-batable that the scarf was the cause of their fame.

Throughout this book, we have shown many different styles of wearing scarves. But the next time you tie a scarf, maybe you should consider this: a scarf is the only garment designed by a famous name that allows you to decide how to wear it. Adding your own brand of chic is the fun part.

Above left: The photographer Horst wearing his signature navy and white polka dot ascot.

Left: Jean Cocteau wearing a large wool challis shawl as a scarf.

Opposite: Fritz Lang with a wool scarf flung over his shoulder.

Page 104: Elsie de Wolfe has moved the scarf knot from under her chin to off on the side of her neck.

Page 105: Gertrude Stein tied her scarf with a loose granny knot and slipped the ends under her blouse.

Above: To achieve this look, place the scarf flat and fold it into a strip about 3 inches wide. Tie it loosely around the neck, but don't knot it.

Opposite: Even more casual is Colette's soft draping of her scarf.

Above right: This begins with a bun and the scarf folded into a triangle. Place the triangle over the bun and wind the two ends down then up and down again. Tie a knot over the bottom flap of the triangle and tuck the end of the flap under or over the center of the knot.

Overleaf left: Another triangle. This time, center the triangle across the neck. Cross the ends behind the neck and back to the front. Adjust the folds and tie a loose double knot.

Overleaf right: Tie this as you would a man's tie. To make the required shape, fold opposite ends of the scarf toward the center repeatedly.

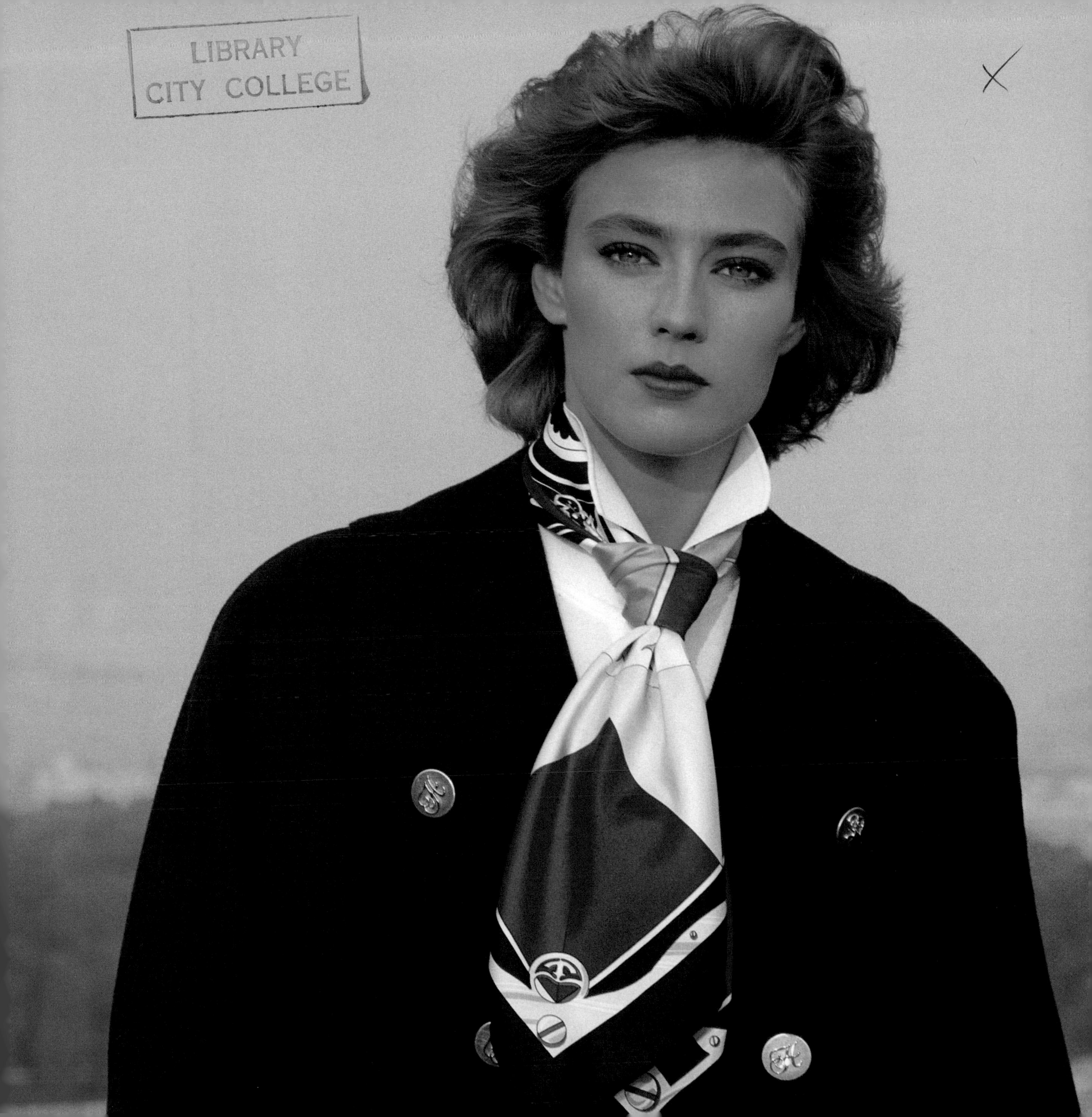

Photo Credits

Page 3: Courtesy Hermès of Paris, Inc.

4 (bottom right): © Horst; *(top right):* Scarf courtesy Metropolitan Museum of Art

5 (top left): Scarf courtesy the Museum of the City of New York; *(top right):* Scarf courtesy Georgina von Etzdorf Archives; *(bottom right):* © Willy Maywald—ADAGP/PARIS

9: Culver Pictures

11: © Horst

13: Courtesy *Vogue.* Copyright © 1925 (renewed 1953) by Condè Nast Publications, Inc.

15: Photograph by Louise Dahl Wolfe/courtesy The Edward C. Blum Design Laboratory, F.I.T., NY

16: Scarves courtesy Georgina von Etzdorf. Modeled by Katherine Roberts; styled by Joanna Silverblatt; hair and make-up by Wess Berlyn for Chameleon, New York. Dress *(top left)* courtesy Michael Kors. Dress *(top right and bottom)* courtesy Anne Klein

18 (top), 19: Photo by Josh Haskin/ courtesy Tiffany & Co.

20 (left): Culver Pictures

20 (right), 21, 22 (left): The Kobal Collection

22 (right): Culver Pictures

23: The Kobal Collection

26 (top left, bottom right): Scarf courtesy Collection of Lynne Wiener; *(top right):* Scarf courtesy Metropolitan Museum of Art

27: Scarf courtesy Metropolitan Museum of Art

32 (left): The Kobal Collection

32 (right): Culver Pictures

33, 34, 35 (both), 36, 37: The Kobal Collection

38: Courtesy The George Zeno Collection

39 (both): The Kobal Collection

40: Culver Pictures

41 (bottom left): Scarf courtesy Echo Design Group Archives

42 (bottom left): Culver Pictures; *(right):* Scarf courtesy Metropolitan Museum of Art

43 (bottom right): Culver Pictures

44 (top left): courtesy Collection of Robert Heide and John Gilman

47 (top left): Scarf courtesy Metropolitan Museum of Art; *(bottom left):* Scarf courtesy Echo Design Group Archives; *(bottom right):* Scarf courtesy Collection of Robert Heide and John Gilman

49 (left): Photograph by Louise Dahl Wolfe/courtesy The Edward C. Blum Design Laboratory, F.I.T., NY; *(right, third from top):* Scarf courtesy Collection of Joan Lang

50, 51 (all): Courtesy Hermès of Paris, Inc.

52 (top left and right, bottom left), 53 (both): Courtesy Hermès of Paris, Inc.

58, 59: Scarves courtesy Echo Design Group Archives

66: Scarf courtesy Collection of Hilary Knight

67: courtesy Collection of Stephen de Pietri

69 (top left): Scarf courtesy Collection of Thomas Oatman for New Republic

70, 71: Scarves courtesy Collection of Karen Kriendler Nelson

72: Jockey courtesy Collection of Joan Lisa

76 (top left): © Willy Maywald—ADAGP/PARIS

79: Photograph © by Louise Dahl Wolfe

80 (bottom): Scarf courtesy Collection of Lynne Wiener

83 (right): The Kobal Collection

86 (left): Courtesy Collection of Jose Pouso

87 (top left): Scarf courtesy Metropolitan Museum of Art

Mary Sykes in Puerto Rico.

89: Scarf courtesy Collection of Bill Cererra

92 (top right): Scarf courtesy Collection of Hakan Rosenius; *(bottom, both):* Scarves courtesy Collection of Paul Smith

95 (top left): Scarf courtesy Collection of Lisa Rich; *(top right):* Scarf courtesy Metropolitan Museum of Art

102 (top): Photo by Robert Farber/ courtesy Horst Studio; *(bottom):* Photograph © Louise Dahl Wolfe

103: Photo by UFA © The Mansell Collection

104: Photograph © by Louise Dahl Wolfe

105: © Horst

106: Culver Pictures

107 (both), 108, 109: Courtesy Hermès of Paris, Inc.

110, 111: Photographs © Louise Dahl Wolfe

112: © Horst

back cover (top left): Courtesy Hermès of Paris, Inc.; *(bottom left):* Scarf courtesy Georgina von Etzdorf Archives

Acknowledgements

I would like to thank the following people who provided vital information, endless support and put up with years of scarf talk: Marilyn and Arnold Baseman of Bird Cage Antiques, Susan Biegen, Bill Cererra, Barbara Corvino of Tiffany & Co., Stephen de Pietri, Michael Dillon, Jonathan Docherty, Stephen Earle, Diana Edkins of Condè Nast, Karen Evans, Lynn Felsher of the Fashion Institute of Technology, Kim Fink of the Metropolitan Museum of Art, Nickie and Jerry Frankel of Pax Antiques, John Gilman and Robert Heide, Lynn Given, Jennifer Gramb, Jacqueline Herald, Drew Hodges of Spot Design, Jonathan Holt, Horikoshi New York, Ginny Jenkins and Hakan Rosenius of Paul Smith, Carol Southern Keneas, Hilary Knight, Peter Kriendler and Karen Kriendler Nelson, Joan Lang, Arthur Lindo and Gillian Moss of the Cooper-Hewitt Museum, Jean Lisa, Rea Lubar and Jan McLatchie of Rea Lubar Inc., Phyllis Magdison of the Museum of the City of New York, Steve Mensch, Thomas Oatman, Anastasia Piper of Gucci, Joan Reil of Vera, Lisa Rich, Tim Rich, Dorothy Roberts of Echo, Michael Rosen of The Thurber House, Shirley Selkin, Ed Seltzer, Jodi Shields, J.C. Suarès, Libby Sunderland of Hermès of Paris, Inc., Georgina von Etzdorf, Mark Walsh, Lynne Wiener, Neil Winkel of Fischbach Gallery, and especially Bertha Fiegenberg, Jo-Ann Early, and Pam and Jim Grumbach.

A special thanks to all the artists and their representatives who participated in the Artists' Scarf Auction, and to everyone at Stewart, Tabori & Chang, including Sarah Longacre, Jose Pouso, and Joseph Rutt. I am grateful to my agent, Marian Young, and lastly but certainly not least to my editor, Roy Finamore, who had insight into the world of scarves when most people didn't get it.

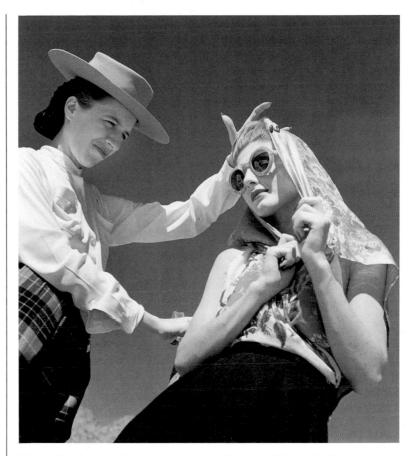

Diana Vreeland styling a photograph of model Bijou (1942).

Design

J.C. Suarès

Joseph Rutt

Composed in Caslon 471, Caslon Old Face, and
Bulmer Italic by Trufont Typographers, Inc., Hicksville,
New York

Printed and bound by
Toppan Printing Company, Ltd.,
Tokyo, Japan